MANNA 101:
THE PREREQUISITE TO THE SCHOOL OF LIFE

"All Glory Goes to God!"

Dontez D. Williams

Unless otherwise indicated scriptures are taken from the King James Version of the Bible.

Quotations marked NLT taken from:
Life Application Study Bible
New Living Translation
Copyright 2004
Tyndale House Publishers, Inc. • Wheaton, IL 60189

© Copyright 2012 Dontez D. Williams

Published By:
MySheri Enterprises, LLC
Detroit, Michigan

ISBN 978-0-97667-822-9

All rights reserved.

No part of this publication may be reproduced, stored in a retrieval system, or transmitted in any form or by means, electronic, mechanical, photocopying, recording or otherwise, without the prior permission of the author.

Permission to reproduce in any part must be obtained in writing from:

Dontez D. Williams
P.O. Box 141111
Detroit, Michigan 48214
www.savedbygracecm.org

Cover Design & Interior Design By:
Sow Graphics & Publications, LLC | Detroit, Michigan

TABLE OF CONTENTS

WELCOME TO MANNA 101	5
THE SEASON OF MANNA	13
THE PURPOSE OF MANNA	29
MY TESTIMONY	41
I WILL TRUST IN THE LORD	55
BECOMING A GOOD STEWARD	67
I KNOW HOW TO ABOUND & BE ABASED	71
I'M NOT IN EGYPT ANYMORE?	77
NOW I CAN DEPEND ON GOD	89
DON'T GIVE UP AT THE BORDER OF THE PROMISED LAND	101
GRADUATION FROM MANNA 101	105
JESUS IS THAT MANNA	111
EPILOGUE	119

CHAPTER ONE

WELCOME TO MANNA 101

"And when the children of Israel saw it, they said one to another, It is manna: for they wist not what it was. And Moses said unto them, This is the bread which the LORD hath given you to eat."
Exodus 16:15

Imagine for a moment that you're walking to school, book bag in hand on a warm summer's day with the sun shining on your back. You're running late and it's your first day, meanwhile you're anxious. You're approaching a large building that forces you to look up at the sign that reads THE SCHOOL OF LIFE. Following the crowd, you walk into the big beautiful doors. Your mind wanders for a moment thinking about all of the people who have entered into these doors. You walk the halls and think of all those who the school has graduated, imagining all the great things the graduates have gone on to do.

In the hallway you approach a security guard who asks to see your ID and schedule. He says, "I'm sorry to inform you that you are in the wrong building. There's a prerequisite that you must complete prior to entering into this school."

You wonder what this class could be. What class haven't you taken? You go over the course requirements and everything seems to be in order. You really can't understand why you aren't ready to attend The School of Life. What class is missing?

You are directed to a road and on that road you get scared because on this road you see everything you never wanted to see. You observe famine, lack and no prosperity in sight. As you travel the road for a while you begin to get cold. You then notice there's snow and not much grass.

You walk up to an old one-room schoolhouse with the door partially off the hinges and the windows are boarded up. You walk into the building and look around the dark room. There's one light, which rests above the chalkboard and in the shadow you see a tall dark figure that you assume is the teacher. The room is so dark you can't even see around you. You suppose you're all alone being the only student in this class. How could you miss this class and why are you the only student? You're trying so hard to remember the course you missed.

Why are you in this class? Why has everything changed? You look around at your situation and wonder…

what have you done to deserve this? You ask yourself, "What are you doing here?" You don't even know what class you're in. Suddenly, you hear footsteps and see a figure out of the shadow. The teacher picks up the chalk and you're anxiously anticipating what the teacher is about to do or say. You don't know what is going to happen at this moment. The teacher writes on the board in big dark letters MANNA 101 and suddenly you remember this is the one class you missed.

This is the one course you were dreading. You never thought you would ever have to take it. You look through your course requirements and you look at the classes you've taken. You're hoping there is another course equivalent to this one.

You find out that there is no other class you can take. You sit in your chair not knowing how long this class is going to take, what is required for this class or when the assignments are due. As you're sitting there it hits you and you remember what the guard said mentioning this course as a prerequisite. It dawns on you: MANNA 101 is The

Prerequisite to the School of Life!

Sinking into your seat, you listen to the teacher as she outlines the course objectives along with a battery of demands. You heard about this class and you promised yourself you would never enroll in it, so throughout the years you did everything you could to avoid taking this class. You glance at your syllabus and you see in the bottom left hand corner MANNA 101 and notice there is a faint check mark there. Perhaps this was to fool yourself into thinking you had taken this class, but the reality kicks in and you realize you never took it and now it's your turn.

You remember people talking about it and telling you how hard it was. So you prepare yourself for a long journey, knowing now that the only way to get into The School of Life is to complete this course. With that thought, you sit back and listen as your teacher wraps up her introduction she says, "Welcome to Manna 101."

Manna is what the children of Israel ate while they were in the wilderness on the way to the Promised Land.

> *John 6:31 Our fathers did eat manna in the desert; as it is written, He gave them bread from heaven to eat.*

After studying this chapter, I've dubbed this period in the children of Israel's history as Manna 101. In my opinion, this is a class Israel was enrolled in for a reason.

> *Deuteronomy 8:16 Who fed thee in the wilderness with manna, which thy fathers knew not, that he might humble thee, and that he might prove thee, to do thee good at thy latter end;*

I believe that there is an awesome testimony behind the Manna. It was through the manna that the Lord proved His word to the children of Israel.

> *Exodus 16:4 Then said the LORD unto Moses, Behold, I will rain bread from heaven for you; and the people shall go out and gather a certain rate every day, that I may prove them, whether they will walk in my law, or no.*

God used the manna to test or to prove the children of Israel. I believe that there are many of us who can relate to the children of Israel as they went through the wilderness.

There are times in our lives when we find ourselves just like the children of Israel: in the Wilderness. We find ourselves eating manna in the morning and quails in the evening and we like the children of Israel ask, "What is this?" This is what we are going discuss throughout this book: God's miraculous keeping power. He is Jehovah Jireh for He is our provider. Through this book we will learn the purpose of manna in our lives and will continue to look into Manna 101. Hopefully, everyone will be able to pass the test.

WELCOME TO MANNA 101

CHAPTER TWO

THE SEASON OF MANNA

"And had rained down manna upon them to eat, and had given them of the corn of heaven."

Psalm 78:24

I propose to you today that there are times in your life when God wants to send you manna to live on and manna alone. Many times in our lives we are faced with times of great need. I can contest that there have been times in my life where I had just enough. It seems to me that sometimes Christians have it a little harder than others. It's almost as if once we get saved the battle begins.

However, this is just a trick of the enemy who would have us think that on his side there is victory, when actually victory is in the name of Jesus! We have a just God. Our Lord is sovereign over all. The truth is that the rain falls on the just and unjust and this is the answer to the age old question, "Why does bad things happen to good people or moreover why do good things happen to bad people?" Let's read…

> *Matthew 5:45 That ye may be the children of your Father which is in heaven: for he maketh his sun to rise on the evil and on the good, and sendeth rain on the just and on the unjust.*

We find in this scripture that the Lord allows the sun to rise on the evil and the good and sends the rain to fall on the just as well as unjust. I can remember when I wasn't saved and I thank God that He allowed the rain to fall on me, otherwise I probably would have never come to the realization that it was time to live holy. So, God must allow the rain to fall on everyone to prove He is a just and loving God.

Even in light of Matthew 5:45, we as Christians think that once we have given our lives over to Christ and we begin to live a saved and holy life that all the trouble will end. We believe that once we begin to walk with the Lord that the sun will always shine. Now trust me, walking with the Lord is better than walking with the devil any day. The Lord's 401K is awesome and the commission checks are bountiful! The devil's pension plan is terrible! The devil has us thinking that the Lord is supposed to stop bad things from happening to us, but I have news for you… as long as you are living you will have attacks from the enemy. It's not a matter of will you go through but how will you go through?

> **1Peter 4:12-13** [12] ***Beloved, think it not strange concerning the fiery trial which is to try you, as though some strange thing happened unto you:*** [13] ***But rejoice, inasmuch as ye are partakers of Christ's sufferings; that, when his glory shall be revealed, ye may be glad also with exceeding joy.***

Peter tells us not to think it strange concerning the fiery trial, which is to try you. He even goes on to say, if I could paraphrase, "Don't act brand new!" In other words, this is the life that you have chosen when you chose to walk with the Lord. When you became a friend of God you instantly became an enemy of the world. You automatically became a fugitive and an outcast in this world. This is why you should no longer look for the world to take care of you. The truth is that the world takes care of its own.

It's amazing to see the friends you have when you are in sin. They seem like they will always be there for you. Then as soon as you get saved your so-called friends leave you. When you begin to live a holy life and no longer walk after the flesh but after the Spirit, you have to lean on God for your needs. You have to begin to trust in the Lord with all your heart. When your family isn't there for you the Lord will be there for you. I heard someone say, "He's a friend." God is the best friend you could ever ask for. Walking with the Lord is an amazing thing. I have to stop and say, "Thank you Jesus!"

So, if you prefer to be a friend of the world you are an enemy of God's.

> *James 4:4 Ye adulterers and adulteresses, know ye not that the friendship of the world is enmity with God? whosoever therefore will be a friend of the world is the enemy of God.*

Now I don't know about you but I don't want to be an enemy of God. I've read in too many places about the enemy of God's and I will tell you that none of them are doing well today! If we be Abraham's seed, saved, sanctified and filled with the Holy Ghost, why do we think that the world owes us anything? We have to step out on the faith of our forefather

Abraham and go to a land whose maker and builder is God.

> **Hebrews 11:10 For he looked for a city which hath foundations, whose builder and maker is God.**

We need to wake up and smell the coffee and trust me it's not decaf! This stuff will wake you up! I have some news for you... the world owes you nothing and even if they did they wouldn't give it to you anyway. This is why the wealth of the wicked is laid up for the just. God has to hand it over to you because they aren't willingly giving it up.

I believe this is the lesson the Lord wants to teach us and has already taught some of us. Some of you reading this book will begin to see what the Lord was doing with you in your life. I believe in my spirit that there are many who have been faced with the attacks of the enemy trying to tell you that the Lord does not love you because of your situation. I am here to tell you that God loves you and the reason you are or were in that situation is because He is conditioning you. He is preparing you for the battle, which is the School of

Life. Tell the devil to get out of your mind. There is a battle going on and victory is in the name of Jesus!

As I said there are times in our lives when we find ourselves eating only manna. I like to call this The Manna Season! This is the season we will be discussing throughout this book. Through the manna season I believe the Lord wants His people to lean not to their own understanding.

> ***Proverbs 3:5 Trust in the LORD with all thine heart; and lean not unto thine own understanding.***

Notice the scripture says to trust in the Lord with all thine heart and lean not to your own understanding. This means you don't question God. You don't look at what the Lord is doing and open up a rap session to figure out what God is doing. You don't need to ask other people what God is doing in your life or try to figure it out yourself. Just know that He is working.

You must begin to take God at His word and eat His word daily. When you truly trust in the Lord you will begin to step out on faith and others will think you are crazy because the world doesn't have faith. Well should I say they don't have faith in God? They have faith in their little gods. Oftentimes, they make themselves gods and things like money, sex and wealth. The world believes that they are the ones doing it. I love the word because it already answers that question.

> *Deuteronomy 8:18 But thou shalt remember the LORD thy God: for it is he that giveth thee power to get wealth, that he may establish his covenant which he sware unto thy fathers, as it is this day.*

God says even if you think you haven't received your blessings from me I was the one who gave you the power to get the wealth you have. When we understand that money and prosperity does not mean holiness or godliness we can start to get in line with the word and receive His blessings.

> *1Timothy 6:5-6 ⁵ Perverse disputings of men of corrupt minds, and destitute of the truth, supposing that gain is godliness: from such withdraw thyself. ⁶ But godliness with contentment is great gain.*

The word teaches us that gain is not godliness all the time. Be careful when you are in your manna season, that is when you are supernaturally being provided for, not to look at what others have or you may find yourself like Asaph.

> *Psalm 73:1-3 ¹ Truly God is good to Israel, even to such as are of a clean heart. ² But as for me, my feet were almost gone; my steps had well nigh slipped. ³ For I was envious at the foolish, when I saw the prosperity of the wicked.*

Our good friend Asaph said that while he was looking at the prosperity of the wicked his feet were almost gone, his steps had almost slipped. What was he saying? I almost backslid; other translations say, "I almost lost faith." Faith is the one thing that you must keep during your manna season. The devil wants you to lose faith, which is why he will have you looking at the prosperity of the wicked. He will try to have you coveting the things of the world. Don't fall for this trick. In the first chapter, we found ourselves in Manna 101 alone, a true indication that in your manna season it is between you and God. I'm getting excited because this is delivering someone as we speak.

What we do in Manna 101 will no doubt benefit us for the rest of our life. It's how we respond to the adversity and trials that show us who we really are. There is no doubt in my mind that in order for us to graduate from Manna 101 and attend the School of Life we must pass a few tests.

Recall the little widow of Zarephath. She was in what I like to call the manna season. She had just enough food for her and her son. Isn't that how it is with us sometimes? When we are in our manna season it seems like we have just enough for us. There's no room to share. This is the time that you need to sow as much as you can and by all means tithe, give offerings and sacrifices! It was tithing that got me through the droughts of my life along with the seeds I've sown in Jesus name!

The word of the Lord came upon Elijah saying that there would not be rain or dew in the land…

> *1Kings 17:1-7 [1] And Elijah the Tishbite, who was of the inhabitants of Gilead, said unto Ahab, As the LORD God of Israel liveth, before whom I stand, there shall not be dew nor rain these years, but according to my word. [2] And the word of the LORD came unto him, saying, [3] Get thee hence, and turn thee eastward, and hide thyself by the brook Cherith, that is before Jordan. [4] And it shall be, that thou shalt drink of the brook; and I have commanded the ravens to feed thee there. [5] So he went and did according unto the word of the LORD: for he went and dwelt by the brook Cherith, that is before Jordan. [6] And the ravens brought him bread and flesh in the morning, and bread and flesh in the evening; and he drank of the brook. [7] And it came to pass after a while, that the brook dried up, because there had been no rain in the land.*

Elijah was in his manna season also and the Lord sustained him. Does this remind you of the children of Israel and how they were sustained by manna and quails? The Lord told him where to go to be fed and to be sustained. The Lord will always give us direction, which ensures that our walk through the wilderness is God ordained.

Keep in mind that the rain falls on the just and the unjust so when the brook dried up what do you think Elijah did? I can tell you that some of us would have cursed God and died, but I have news for you… when we do that we automatically flunk Manna 101 and have to reenroll! Let's find out what Elijah did:

> *1 Kings 17:9-10 Arise, get thee to Zarephath, which belongeth to Zidon, and dwell there: behold, I have commanded a widow woman there to sustain thee [10] So he arose and went to Zarephath. And when he came to the gate of the city, behold, the widow woman was there gathering of sticks: and he called to her, and said, Fetch me, I pray thee, a little water in a vessel, that I may drink.*

The widow here was deep in her manna season. When we understand that the widow already didn't have much, we understand that she was living in her manna season. So, Elijah had to have faith to believe that a widow could sustain him. How many know that in Manna 101 there are pop quizzes? In fact the final exam is easier than all the tests throughout the course of the class. Let's look at one of the widow's quizzes in Manna 101.

> *1Kings 17:11-14 [11] And as she was going to fetch it, he called to her, and said, Bring me, I pray thee, a morsel of bread in thine hand. [12] And she said, As the LORD thy God liveth, I have not a cake, but an handful of meal in a barrel, and a little oil in a cruse: and, behold, I am gathering two sticks, that I may go in and dress it for me and my son, that we may eat it, and die. [13] And Elijah said unto her, Fear not; go and do as thou hast said: but make me thereof a little cake first, and bring it unto me, and after make for thee and for thy son. [14] For thus saith the LORD God of Israel, The barrel of meal shall not waste, neither shall the cruse of oil fail, until the day that the LORD sendeth rain upon the earth.*

Isn't this quite a test for the widow? Previously she told the prophet that all she had was enough for one more meal for her and her son and then they'd both starve to death. Notice what the prophet tells her; give unto him the food first. God was testing her faith because she could have easily replied, "no" and been justified. After all she was in her manna season and all she had was "enough". She had just enough for one more meal, and then they were going to die.

How would you respond to the prophet if you were in this situation? How do you respond to your Pastor's appeal for the light or gas bill when you just received your bills? In the manna season it is very important to know how to respond to the situation. God was setting her up for a blessing. Notice the prophet tells her that the oil and meal will never run out so long as there is drought throughout the land. God was basically saying as you are going through the wilderness I will give you Manna, revealing that the Lord will honor our sacrifice. I declare that if you give to God He will give it back to you; good measure, pressed down, shaken together and running over. [Luke 6:38] You can't out-give God, trust me! Let's see how the widow responded to the prophet Elijah:

> **1Kings 17:15-16** **¹⁵ *And she went and did according to the saying of Elijah: and she, and he, and her house, did eat many days. ¹⁶ And the barrel of meal wasted not, neither did the cruse of oil fail, according to the word of the LORD, which he spake by Elijah.***

Praise the Lord! We find that the word of the prophet was true and the widow did as she was instructed, with God honoring her obedience. I declare she put her whole trust in the Lord and found herself among the graduates of Manna 101. The Lord supernaturally sustained her through her manna season while others were suffering.

The Lord wants to do this same thing for you. I know that the Lord has done this for me. It was in my manna season that the Lord begin to deal with me regarding writing this book. I felt in my spirit that though I was enrolled in Manna 101 and couldn't see anyone else I trusted that there were other people in the class with me. I also knew that there were others out there who would be watching me. In fact, I felt that one day I would become a tutor in the class. Like that widow, my oil never ran out. Even to this day, I am astonished at how the Lord sustained me. Thank you Jesus!

I guess by now you have figured out what I mean by manna season. I'm talking about the periods in your life when you thought you were on your way to the Promised Land and you found yourself in the wilderness where the Lord had to begin feeding you manna. I'm talking about those times when you didn't have food in your refrigerator, but miraculously you ate three full meals every day. I'm talking to the people who the Lord had to sustain until a change came. I'm talking to the widows who sacrificed their last meal as unto the Lord and you found that your meal and oil never ran out. If you're one of these people you can relate to me. I declare this is a class everyone has to take. If you have never been enrolled in Manna 101, pay close attention because soon you will be registered.

We're going to look at the purpose of manna in the next chapter and see exactly what I believe manna is and what it represents.

Chapter Three

The Purpose of Manna

"And Moses and Aaron said unto all the children of Israel, At even, then ye shall know that the LORD hath brought you out from the land of Egypt:"

Exodus 16:6

The Lord began to give me revelation of what manna really is and what it is meant for. The truth is, I believe manna is more of a lesson than anything else. When we think about the children of Israel they were in captivity in Egypt for a long time. They were fed and taken care of by the Egyptians. Their whole existence consisted of what the Egyptians gave them. I hear the Lord saying,

"While you were in the world the world took care of you but now you are in me and I have to show you what it truly means to be taken care of. The world will care for you only while you are with them. I am a sustainer and will tend to all your needs. I know what you need before you ask".

We as Christians get so comfortable in thinking this trip is going to be an easy one, that the journey through life is going to be a walk in the park and we'll make it through without a hitch. I have news for you… there will be troubles.

Job 14:1 Man that is born of a woman is of few days, and full of trouble.

The bible never gives us a certificate of exemption from the troubles of this world. We must learn to embrace our manna period. This probably isn't a popular subject, but it is one that must be spread. The fact is that I believe God is giving lessons in life to many of us Christians. I can honestly say I am near to the top of the class.

When it came time for my manna season I was shocked and surprised that it had fallen on me. I never thought I would find myself in the situations I was in. This period for me didn't come when I was walking according to the ways of this world, but after I began to walk holy and upright before Him. Like Job, I was doing nothing and trouble still came.

There have been periods in my Christian life when I literally didn't have a dime in my pocket. I needed gas and I prayed and someone would give me $20.00. I didn't understand it because I wasn't used to driving my car on anything but a full tank. I would go to the gas station and fill up 2 to 3 times a week if I had to. You could ask anyone and they'll tell you I would drive all day long and never complain about gas money. I was once told that I was a Detroit Taxi.

However, when God enrolled me in the class I like to call: Manna 101, I was in for a rude awakening. The Lord began to deal with me regarding all the things I had been doing in my life.

All the money mismanagements, friends I had acquired and almost every aspect of my walk in the Lord. I began to see that one of the crucial pieces I was missing was my manna season.

I began to feel like the children of Israel. I had to go through the Wilderness of Sin. Isn't that a funny name for the wilderness? Isn't that how it is for most of us? We have to go through that wilderness and even in the midst of that wilderness we continue to sin and make everything worse. We may not take 40 years to complete a short journey but we do make things a lot harder on ourselves than they should be. Why do we do this? Because we are not trusting in the Lord with all our hearts, but we are continuing to lean on our own understanding.

The truth is that when we really begin to let God move in our lives He can take care of everything. By the time you are deep in your Manna season your whole outlook on life begins to change. You begin to see the superficiality of the things you are doing, what is important and what is not. Everything comes into perspective.

The purpose of your manna season is to show you that you are no longer in Egypt. It proves you're on the right path and that you're on your way to the Promised Land. So, rejoice in the Lord and don't give up, your Promised Land is a few days away and by faith believe that. Receive that and say amen!

The sad part about human beings is that we have to go through something before we are prepared to talk about it. What am I saying? We as people tend not to believe a person unless they've been through the thing they are talking about. There is no difference with Jesus. He was tempted just like us, but never sinned. Here's the reason He can say, "Be holy for I am holy."

> *Hebrews 4:15 For we have not an high priest which cannot be touched with the feeling of our infirmities; but was in all points tempted like as we are, yet without sin.*

I can understand the importance of the many classes our Professor God offers to us as Christians. There are so many lessons we need to learn to be made ready for the mission He has assigned us. The truth is, it is more dangerous to send a soldier out unprepared than it is to be short a soldier. That one unprepared soldier may destroy the whole regiment. It is dangerous to send a baby into the battlefield. Unfortunately, this reflects how many of us are today: babies in the battlefield.

The same thing is true with our faith. It's important in our manna season to surround ourselves with people who have the faith and not only have the faith, but they're keeping the faith. All throughout the bible we see occasions when people lost the faith. These are the people I don't need to hang around. If I am in my manna season why do I need someone helping me to complain or murmur?

God knows what He is doing in your life. I feel in my Spirit that there are many of us Christians who are in our manna season. The encouragement I have for you is, don't worry! God is going to see you through. The same God that delivered you out of divers temptations and troubles will deliver you from your manna season. You must believe me when I tell you that there is a lesson within the breaking of the manna. There is a message God is trying to get to you. It may be that the things you had were stopping you from hearing. Oftentimes to grab your attention, God will allow the distractions to be removed from your life.

When the Lord began to allow things to be taken from me I was a little upset. Well, let me not lie... I was totally upset. I began to murmur and complain because after all I was not used to this. I wasn't used to not having money in my pockets, not being able to do what I wanted to do or filling up my tank twice in one day if I had to. I wasn't used to looking at the fuel gauge to see how many miles I could go before I ran out.

Before my manna season I couldn't tell you what the low fuel light in my car looked like. I can tell you this though, while in my manna season I saw that light plenty of times. There were many times I had to navigate through traffic, while praying there wouldn't be a traffic jam, so that I would have enough gas to get to where I was going. But thank God I got there!

That season of my life has given me a great outlook on the things of this world and what really matters the most. My wife and I pressed through it all and continued to keep the faith and we did what had to be done for God. I had never done manual labor and even found myself working for temporary agencies. I mean I would come home filthy. In all this I gave God the glory, because I began to understand what the Lord was doing in my life. There were some things in me that needed to come out. There were hidden faults that I had never identified and the manna season brought it out.

One of the reasons for the manna season is to bring out things about you that you didn't realize were inside you. *Some of the things and attitudes picked up in Egypt have to be humbled out of you.* We are no longer in Egypt and we can't expect to live the way we were. We have to begin to learn how to live off of God's provision and not Pharaoh's. Pharaoh receives no glory and God does! After all Pharaoh drowned in the Red Sea.

Without the comforts you are used to, you begin to see the things that really bothered you. You begin to see that you were simply masking the troubles of this world with the makeup of this world called "things". We know that life does not consist in the abundance of things.

> ***Luke 12:15 And he said unto them, Take heed, and beware of covetousness: for a man's life consisteth not in the abundance of the things which he possesseth.***

This is why there are many millionaires who kill

themselves. But I praise the Lord that before He began to give me everything in abundance He took me through my manna season. He took everything away so that I would gain appreciation.

The Lord began to show me that my life was like a junkie garage. I had so many things in it that needed to be removed in order for me to receive more. It's hard for us to understand that when all we can see is our Cadillac being taken away. We don't believe that God is making room in the driveway for our Bentley while they're towing our Cadillac away! That takes great faith, and when you are in the manna season you will see faith like you have never seen.

In my manna season I couldn't find a steady job. It looked like all the things I was doing was not producing any results and this was uncommon for me. I was able to do whatever I put my mind to. It was when I started to see that God was the one in charge, I stopped asking questions. I began to expect things from God. I knew when I was in a tight situation God had obligated himself to take care of me.

After all I was His child and He promised me that He would take care of me.

Everything I learned about faith began to show itself to me. The words on the pages of my bible began to come true right before my eyes and I could see myself being cared for in ways I had never thought of. In the midst of a fiery trial I saw and felt myself turning into GOLD! Praise the Lord for that.

It's a really good feeling to know that the trouble you are going through is making you a better person. My God, I can truly say I appreciate it more now, than I ever have.

Here's yet another lesson that is taught through the season of manna. We learn how to appreciate things more because of what we have been through. If you listen to anyone who is rich and famous now, they will contest that they too found themselves in their manna season.

They may not call it that, but I guarantee you their experience was similar to the class called Manna 101.

Chapter Four

My Testimony

"And they overcame him by the blood of the Lamb, and by the word of their testimony; and they loved not their lives unto the death"
Revelation 12:11

MY TESTIMONY

I have to say looking back at all that I have been through in my life, "God has been good to me!" I remember when I was enrolled in the class I have so much referred to as Manna 101. I thought I was well on my way to the School of Life with my bible in hand prepared to spread the good news. I had been in the Lord for a while and I thought it was time for me to shine.

I'd been preaching at a church and you couldn't have told me that I wasn't on my way to becoming a mega preacher. I was wrong. I, like so many of you, found myself in the same situation as we did in chapter one. Being grabbed by the security guard and told that I was in the wrong place.

For me, my manna season was to help me to believe more in God and build my faith. I had a man tell me that my faith in God was shaky. That was to say that I would believe God and then not believe God. It's something to be able to declare something and not believe it. I was in that place. I could tell you that God can do all types of things but I couldn't experience it for myself. I was like a chef who was allergic to food. I could prepare all types of dishes but I couldn't eat them. I found myself in a position where I was walking with the Lord and preaching His Word and I myself wasn't living right. I needed to be taught again.

> *Hebrews 5:12 For when for the time ye ought to be teachers, ye have need that one teach you again which be the first principles of the oracles of God; and are become such as have need of milk, and not of strong meat.*

So, it comes to me now as no surprise that I was enrolled in Manna 101. It happened for me when I got married. People thought that we were crazy. Neither of us had a full time job. I had just about enough money to buy the ring and maybe a few meals. However, when I met my wife for the first time I saw that she was the one I would enter into the Promised Land with. I had supposed we were on our way to peace and prosperity. However it was soon after that the Lord had enrolled both of us in Manna 101. I know now we both had to endure the wilderness together because we would be in the Promised Land together, which is what the children of Israel didn't realize. They all had to go through the same things. They had to eat of God's Manna because they were going to be partaking of the overflow in the Promised Land. So, I knew that my wife was the one because she endured the wilderness journey with me.

Looking back, things were not that bad, but we suffered in the flesh. We had to go without a lot. The Lord really proved himself faithful to us. It was through this wilderness experience that I began to see the faith of the bird. The bible teaches us that the bird doesn't worry about what to eat or when he will eat, but God feeds him. It's the most wonderful and profound thing that the Lord says that if He feeds the fouls of the air won't He feed you? I could see that I was acquiring the faith of a bird. I began to see that the Lord was faithful despite my shortcomings and what the Grace of God really meant in my life. We began to see that the Lord had indeed promised us the good of the land if we were obedient. [Isaiah 1:9]

Even though we did suffer in the flesh I held fast to the word and knew that if I was suffering in the flesh I had ceased from sin.

> **1Peter 4:1 Forasmuch then as Christ hath suffered for us in the flesh, arm yourselves likewise with the same mind: for he that hath suffered in the flesh hath ceased from sin;**

The Lord began to work with me and my wife regarding trusting in Him and Him alone. In the midst of our manna season the Lord sent people into our lives to prophesy to us regarding our future. These people all agreed in the spirit that we were going to be blessed and indeed we were on the right path and had not taken a detour, but was well on our way to the Promised Land. It's hard to consider being told in the midst of the manna season that you are on your way to the Promised Land. The road we started on to Manna 101 was not at all the most beautiful of roads. Even in the midst of all this we held on to our profession of faith. We held on to the word the Lord had sent us. Even now we are seeing the blessings of the Lord come to pass. Thank you Jesus! My wife and I endured battle like soldiers.

> **2 Timothy 2:3 Thou therefore endure hardness, as a good soldier of Jesus Christ.**

We pressed our way to church three times a week and we didn't back down like others would have done. When the devil told us we shouldn't go, we went earlier. We knew that the only way out of the wilderness was to praise the Lord in the midst of it. We had no intentions on making our manna season longer than it needed to be. We knew that in our manna season God was showing us something and that we'd better pay attention. Isn't it funny though that when we are going through something we go to the hospital called the church that there is a fresh word for us? My father-in-law was the Bishop of our church and during that manna season he knew exactly what I was going through. Remember, there is no temptation that isn't common to all men.

> **1 Corinthians 10:13 There hath no temptation taken you but such as is common to man: but God is faithful, who will not suffer you to be tempted above that ye are able; but will with the temptation also make a way to escape, that ye may be able to bear it.**

To this day I thank God that even in my manna season I had enough sense to trust in the Lord. My father-in-law can tell you that not one time in that manna season did I ask for help. I knew the Lord was working some things out of me and my wife. My wife was very spoiled by her parents and both her and her parents know it. We have even joked about it, but this is what our manna season had to bring out of my wife. The Lord had to take her into the wilderness away from the support of her parents, so she could depend on God.

If ever an enemy of mine were to read this book they would say, "Ha, ha, ha." It's quite the contrary, through all of this my wife and I have become so close. The love I have for my wife couldn't compare to anything in this world. Outside of God she's the best thing that has ever happened to me. She is truly my true love. I indeed found true love God's way. It was through our manna season that we began to press our way into the Holy of Holies and commune with the Lord. Not having the money and working the temporary jobs taught me to ration. The manna allowed me to view God as my provider. I learned to take my daily bread and be happy with it. When I had little I was still blessing the Lord. I was still tithing. If I got a dollar I gave a dime. The Lord began to show me the way to the Promised Land, giving me fresh revelations and I knew that I was no longer in Egypt!

There was a time when my car note was due and they threatened to come and get it and a temporary job called me. The recruiter said it would probably last a few weeks, so I went as others did. I worked 5 or 6 days and as I was adding up the money I knew that on the sixth day the job would be over because I had enough for my car note. As sure as the Lord lives on the sixth day they said they didn't need any more help.

What am I saying? I learned to trust in the Lord. I

knew that as long as I had enough money to pay the car note I was fine. While I was in my manna season I didn't have a steady job however, thank you Jesus, my car note and insurance was paid, and I didn't want for anything.

My manna season was the season for me to learn again. I desired to be a teacher, but didn't fully understand the course that I was teaching. I wasn't trained properly for the battle. It's something how the Lord will move you and you find yourself right where you need to be. I had a desire to preach and the irony of that was that the wife the Lord had for me would of all things be a PK [Preacher's Kid]? Isn't God good?

In my manna season, I can honestly say I thank God for my wife, my mother, grandmother, my best friend Jackie, my sister, brother and my mother and father-in-law. These are the people who helped to keep us afloat. I thank my mother for helping us in so many ways. It was the continued love, forgiveness and support my grandmother sowed into my life even in her own manna season. Jackie sowed seeds into my life during my manna season and was obedient to the word of the Lord. During my manna season my in-laws were the best in-laws anyone could ask for. My mother-in-law has said time and time again that she prayed for her children's spouses since they were born. I declare that her prayers have gotten me through a lot. My father-in-law is a dynamic preacher, anointed and appointed by God. In a minute he will tell you, "Jesus is all you need!" I thank him for even in my manna season; he never once interjected in my marriage. He allowed us to go through and be tried in the fire and I declare we're 24 karat gold now!

What am I implying with all of this? Surround yourself with people who can help to build you up in your manna season. The wilderness is no place to play, but I heard God say:

> *Isaiah 43:19 Behold, I will do a new thing; now it shall spring forth; shall ye not know it? I will even make a way in the wilderness, and rivers in the desert.*

I declare God has done a new thing in my life. He made a way in the wilderness for me with a river in my desert. God is good. The Lord will never leave you or forsake you. It was through Manna 101 that I learned so many things. Things I would have never learned had I gone right into the School of Life.

We must understand that the Lord knows what He is doing. The Lord doesn't need our help or input. When we get involved too much that's when bad things start happening. It's when we try to drive, we veer off course. Then as we are on the side of the road with a flat tire and a blown engine we try to give God the steering wheel. Even in that dead and motionless situation God can and will deliver you, if you allow Him to move in your life!

I believe that I am speaking prophetically right now for someone because I believe that you have gone through so much in your life. Before now you didn't know why, but I'm here to tell you that the Lord has tried you in the fire to bring you out as gold. Behold God was in the fire with you. I know He was in the furnace with me.

> *Daniel 3:25 He answered and said, Lo, I see four men loose, walking in the midst of the fire, and they have no hurt; and the form of the fourth is like the Son of God.*

Jesus was right there with me through my manna season. For the first time since I was an adolescent I went without a haircut for over a month. Just as Job lost everything I can say in the flesh I lost everything. Through it all, the Lord sustained me and now I can say I am more than a conqueror.

> *Romans 8:37-39 [37] Nay, in all these things we are more than conquerors through him that loved us. [38] For I am persuaded, that neither death, nor life, nor angels, nor principalities, nor powers, nor things present, nor things to come, [39] Nor height, nor depth, nor any other creature, shall be able to separate us from the love of God, which is in Christ Jesus our Lord.*

While walking through the wilderness you have to believe that with your whole heart. You have to believe that the Lord Jesus Christ is there and that you have the victory in Jesus Name.

This is my testimony and your manna season may be different and bring different results. However, I can say that I am truly a man who God has changed from within. I'm well on my way. I am in the Promised Land! Thank you Jesus!

In the next chapter, we will talk about trusting in the Lord. This will be in your final exam.

MY TESTIMONY

CHAPTER FIVE

I WILL TRUST IN THE LORD

"Offer the sacrifices of righteousness, and put your trust in the LORD."

Psalm 4:5

Another purpose of the Manna season is to teach us to trust in the Lord. Too many times we find ourselves like the children of Israel: eating God's manna but not His word.

> *Matthew 4:4 But he answered and said, It is written, Man shall not live by bread alone, but by every word that proceedeth out of the mouth of God.*

This is why many of us are still hungry after eating all day long. We have not filled up with God's word. We have continually eaten God's manna, but never tasting His word. When you let the Word of God get into your heart and soul you will begin to feel yourself being filled from the inside.

The Lord sent manna to the children of Israel because of their murmuring and complaining.

> *Exodus 16:2-4 ² And the whole congregation of the children of Israel murmured against Moses and Aaron in the wilderness: ³ And the children of Israel said unto them, Would to God we had died by the hand of the LORD in the land of Egypt, when we sat by the flesh pots, and when we did eat bread to the full; for ye have brought us forth into this wilderness, to kill this whole assembly with hunger. ⁴ The said the LORD unto Moses, Behold, I will rain bread from heaven for you; and the people shall go out and gather a certain rate every day, that I may prove them, whether they will walk in my law, or no.*

The children of Israel supposed that they were going to die in the wilderness. They didn't have faith in the Lord. If they had faith they wouldn't have questioned what God was doing. We don't fault the children of Israel because after all they were called children for a reason. The Lord heard their murmuring and decided He would do something about it.

Manna is God's way of proving Himself to us. If God wanted to, He could have not given the children of Israel manna and they still would have been full, but because of their lack of faith, God had to give them outwardly what He could have placed inside of them. The children of Israel ate God's word daily, which is the manna. We are taught today to take God's word into our souls.

God could have fed them without the manna but because of unbelief He had to pour manna from heaven to prove to them that He would feed them. God's word can feed us. Jesus spent 40 days in the wilderness being tempted by the devil eating only God's word. That was His manna season!

Through Jesus' manna season He proved that He had full trust in the Lord. Manna is conditioning you for the battle that is to say the School of Life. This is why this period should be embraced. It is preparing you for life. I thank God for my manna season. It was through it that I learned how to trust in the Lord with all my heart and not lean on my own understanding.

It was through my manna season that I began to

acquire a relationship with the Lord that I thank Him for today. It was through this manna season that my relationship with my wife was strengthened. We are happily married and are looking forward to spending the rest of our lives together! He blessed me with a wife who was willing to go with me through our manna season without the added murmuring and complaining. I thank God for her and my manna season!

When you learn to trust in the Lord you will begin to see yourself moving in a realm that you never thought you would find yourself in. You begin to trust in the Lord with all your heart and more sooner than later you find yourself a graduate of Manna 101 and prepared for life.

You have to understand that during your manna season your faith is on trial. The Lord as well as the devil is standing by to see where your faith is going. Job knew about Manna 101 more than anyone. He lost all his children, his money and his health. He never lost faith in God. In fact, all the people around him thought that he was in trouble, but he knew something we didn't know.

> *Job 2:9-10 ⁹ Then said his wife unto him, Dost thou still retain thine integrity? curse God, and die. ¹⁰ But he said unto her, Thou speakest as one of the foolish women speaketh. What? shall we receive good at the hand of God, and shall we not receive evil? In all this did not Job sin with his lips.*

I thank God I don't have a wife like Job's. She told him to curse God and die. This shows why you need people around you who can tell you to keep your integrity and not to compromise while you are in your manna season. The devil is already telling you to curse God and die and you don't need to hear it coming from your wife.

Job says that if we can receive good from God can't we receive the bad? What was Job saying? "The rain falls on the just and the unjust." Job knew that his manna season wouldn't last forever. Job's faith in his manna season is wonderful. I referred many times to Job in my own manna season because Job's faith in his manna season is an inspiration to anyone in theirs.

> *Job 13:15 Though he slay me, yet will I trust in him: but I will maintain mine own ways before him.*

Though He slay me, yet will I trust in Him. This sounds good to quote, but when we find ourselves in our manna season we don't reflect on this verse of scripture. Through all the things Job went through he maintained his ways before the Lord. Here's where we need to be in our Christian walks, where no matter what comes we maintain a holy standard before the Lord. Trust me, this is one of the purposes of your manna season and that is to build your trust in the Lord.

The children of Israel had no one else they could call on. They murmured about going back to Egypt and bragged about the food they had, when in reality they couldn't have gone back to Egypt if they tried, because the Lord was delivering them out of their bondage. Besides, the Red Sea was parted, so that they could get into the wilderness and make it towards the Promised Land. The children of Israel was delivered miraculously from Egypt, which tells us that the children of Israel couldn't have went back unless it was in God's will and trust me it wasn't. Now in the wilderness they are stuck between a rock and a harder place and they must trust in the Lord.

What do you do when you are confronted with your manna season? Are you like Job or are you like his wife? Is it so easy for you to lose your faith in the almighty? Do you allow things of this world to pull you away from the word of the Lord? If you find yourself always losing faith, I can tell you that you have not completed Manna 101. As long as you are failing Manna 101 you will have to continue to take the course. You have to begin to trust in the Lord with all your heart and embrace your manna periods.

You have to begin to take God at His word.

> ***2 Corinthians 1:20 For all the promises of God in him are yea, and in him Amen, unto the glory of God by us.***

If God has told you that you are going to the Promised Land no matter what it looks like, know that you are going into the Promised Land. No matter if you find yourself on a detour you will get to your Promised Land. We look at our situations and then begin to doubt God. We begin to say that there is no way God can get us out of it, when the truth is God is just waiting to deliver you from yourself, as long as you are willing to be delivered.

When you find yourself as we did in chapter one, enrolled in Manna 101, don't be afraid, but know that the Lord is with you. The Lord is preparing you to walk into your Promised Land.

Don't worry about if you don't know what you are going to do. Do you remember the light over the chalkboard? That is the same light that guided the children of Israel through the wilderness.

> *Exodus 13:21 And the LORD went before them by day in a pillar of a cloud, to lead them the way; and by night in a pillar of fire, to give them light; to go by day and night:*

When we let go and let God lead us we find ourselves

in better situations. The truth is that we don't really start to live until we have gone through that manna season and begin to trust in the Lord. When you trust in the Lord it is easy to say, "Not my will but thy will be done." You begin to see God's will is perfect and you want to walk therein.

I thank God for teaching me to trust in Him. There were times in my manna season when I thought I wouldn't make it and then the Lord would make a way. The Lord proved me and He proved Himself to me. He began to minister to me daily regarding trust. Though I was being broken in the flesh I was being strengthened in the spirit. I thank God for that strengthening in the Holy Ghost. The Lord delivered unto me more power through the Holy Ghost than I had ever received.

> *Acts 1:8 But ye shall receive power, after that the Holy Ghost is come upon you: and ye shall be witnesses unto me both in Jerusalem, and in all Judaea, and in Samaria, and unto the uttermost part of the earth.*

That power can't be compared to anything in this

world. To know that you have the power to tread upon serpents and the power over the prince of the world is an awesome thing. It wasn't until I began to go through my manna season that I began to walk in authority. It was probably because I had no other option. I wasn't going to curse God and I surely wasn't going to lie down and die either. So, I had to hold on and have faith. I began to say to some mountains in my life MOVE and they were moved in Jesus name! My question to you is, do you trust God? Are you learning to trust God? Have you gone through your manna season? I hope you trust in God but if not, your manna season will help you to trust in him.

If you remember the story of the rich man and Lazarus, you will see how a manna season will help you trust in God. The rich man and the beggar Lazarus had an encounter in this life. Lazarus put his trust in the Lord and the rich man put his trust in himself and his riches. When they both find themselves dead, Lazarus is comforted by Abraham, while the rich man is in the place of torment.

Thirsty and hot he pleads to Abraham:

> ***Luke 16:24 And he cried and said, Father Abraham, have mercy on me, and send Lazarus, that he may dip the tip of his finger in water, and cool my tongue; for I am tormented in this flame.***

I don't know about you, but I don't want to wait until I find myself in hell to start believing and trusting in God. I want to do it now while there is still time. Even the rich man began to have faith in the almighty. He even went on to plead on the behalf of his brothers. However, he was unable to get his wish.

We have to stop putting our faith in things and this world. We have to lean more to God. If nothing else will do it, Manna 101 will and that's something you can take to the bank. Remember, God makes the rain to fall on the just and the unjust so just wait for your number… it will be called.

CHAPTER SIX

BECOMING A GOOD STEWARD

"And it shall come to pass, that on the sixth day they shall prepare that which they bring in; and it shall be twice as much as they gather daily."

I propose that through your manna season God is teaching you to manage your life. The manna for the children of Israel was rationed out. They all had to gather enough for just a day. Remember when we talked about having just enough? This is the beginning of your manna season. Having just enough is very important in learning to manage your life again.

Throughout most of our lives we have learned the wrong way to manage our lives? We find ourselves deeper in debt and never really finding a way out of it. We've learned from the world how to manage our lives. When we begin to go through our manna season and God rations out to us and we have just enough, we learn how to appreciate and how to take care of the things we are given.

Now on the sixth day the Lord allowed them to gather enough for two days. This was the children of Israel's first test on management of their new lives. They were being trusted to gather enough food for two days and if they didn't take care of the manna, they wouldn't eat the seventh day.

The Lord was testing their stewardship as well as their trust in Him. The Lord didn't send manna on the seventh day, so in order to eat on the seventh day they had to believe in the word of the Lord. They couldn't just eat His manna but they had to eat His word.

The children of Israel had to be proven whether or not they would observe God's law. They had to prove themselves to God by their faithfulness. This is another purpose for manna and the season; it comes to prove you to God.

> *Matthew 25:21 His lord said unto him, Well done, thou good and faithful servant: thou hast been faithful over a few things, I will make thee ruler over many things: enter thou into the joy of thy lord.*

It's amazing that after you have proven to be a faithful servant God will say to you, "well done!" You must be faithful. When you are faithful God rewards your diligence. God also honors your faith and loves to bless His people.

BECOMING A GOOD STEWARD

Chapter Seven

I Know How To Abound & Be Abased

"I know both how to be abased, and I know how to abound: every where and in all things I am instructed both to be full and to be hungry, both to abound and to suffer need."
Philippians 4:12

There is another very important purpose of our Manna Season. When you read Paul's letter to the Philippians he says that he has learned how to be content in every situation.

> *Philippians 4:11 Not that I speak in respect of want: for I have learned, in whatsoever state I am, therewith to be content.*

What Paul is saying is that he has learned how to be happy knowing that he has a relationship with God. How did he acquire such a relationship and trust in the Lord? I propose it was through his manna season. Why do I say that? Well the next verse that follows proves my point.

> *Philippians 4:12 I know both how to be abased, and I know how to abound: every where and in all things I am instructed both to be full and to be hungry, both to abound and to suffer need.*

Let's look at these verses in the New Living Translation:

> *Philippians 4:11-12 NLT* [11]*Not that I was ever in need, for I have learned how to be content with whatever I have.* [12]*I know how to live on almost nothing or with everything. I have learned the secret of living in every situation, whether it is with a full stomach or empty, with plenty or little.*

Paul was saying he has been through his manna season and it was through that manna season that the Lord showed him the secret of being content. It's easy to praise the Lord when all your bills are paid and there's a few dollars in the bank, but what do you do when you don't have enough gas to get to church? Will you press your way into the house of the Lord? Or will you allow your situation to determine your destiny? I love what Paul says, "I've learned…" This is what our Manna Season does for us… It teaches us to be content with whatever we have.

Paul was an Apostle to the gentiles. We know that Paul was a very well bread man. Let's review a little of Paul's Pedigree:

> *Philippians 3:4-7 ⁴ Though I might also have confidence in the flesh. If any other man thinketh that he hath whereof he might trust in the flesh, I more: ⁵ Circumcised the eighth day, of the stock of Israel, of the tribe of Benjamin, an Hebrew of the Hebrews; as touching the law, a Pharisee; ⁶ Concerning zeal, persecuting the church; touching the righteousness which is in the law, blameless. ⁷ But what things were gain to me, those I counted loss for Christ.*

Paul had this wonderful resume' and still was missing the mark. I believe it was through his manna experience that the Lord had to humble him. One of the purposes of manna is to humble out some of the characters and attitudes picked up in Egypt. Though Paul had these bragging rights, he says he counts it all a lost. Paul was simply saying that everything he thought he was, couldn't compare to what he was going to be in Christ. This is why our manna season is so important. It shows us what we have to work on within ourselves.

There is nothing like a manna season to prepare you for the school of life. I can tell you like Paul, I too had to go through my manna season to humble me. It was through my manna season that I received greater revelation and grew closer to my Lord and Savior. I can say like Paul, I know how to abound and I know how to be abased. I know how to be content in every situation.

What did you do in your manna season? Have you had your manna season? If you did have your manna season can you say like Paul I know how to abound and I know how to be abased? Or are you still scratching your head and trying to figure out why you ever got into this situation? I can testify that what Paul has said is a great thing. To find that you can be content in every situation: That is a blessing from the Lord. We need to live a humble life.

> *1Corinthians 10:12 Wherefore let him that thinketh he standeth take heed lest he fall.*

What was Paul saying? Don't get too caught up with pride thinking it was you or someone you know who got you where you are or you will be humbled. As sure as the summer ends and gives way to the fall, you will have a manna season. You will have your manna season as you are on your way into the Promised Land. If you just found yourself in the wilderness, rejoice because on your divine map, your Promised Land is right on the other side. The fastest way to the Promised Land is through the wilderness.

Thank God that you are going through your manna season, because sooner or later you will be in your Promised Land.

In the next chapter we will discuss why it is a blessing to be eating manna.

Chapter Eight

I'm Not in Egypt Anymore?

"And Moses and Aaron said unto all the children of Israel, At even, then ye shall know that the LORD hath brought you out from the land of Egypt:"

Exodus 16:6

This is something the Lord put in my spirit about my manna season. The Lord began to show me that as long as I was eating manna I was no longer in Egypt. The children of Israel didn't realize that they were really blessed. They began to complain to Moses and Aaron about how they ate in Egypt. They never thought about the fact that in Egypt they were in bondage.

> *Galatians 5:1 Stand fast therefore in the liberty wherewith Christ hath made us free, and be not entangled again with the yoke of bondage.*

If they were to go back to Egypt they would be again in bondage. Paul tells us not to be entangled again with the yoke of bondage. In other words, don't go where you just left. There was a reason you left in the first place. Things weren't that good back there in Egypt!

This is how we start our manna season! We start thinking about all the things we had in the world and that we actually had it better in the world. The devil has us fooled into thinking that our old life was so much better. The truth is, we are being taken care of better now than we ever were.

I believe that through our manna season the Lord begins to work with us through our spirit. He begins to take us through a journey over our whole life, showing us all of our shortcomings. It is through this that we begin to see how Pharaoh had us fooled. The devil had us thinking that there isn't anything wrong with us, but honestly we all need to be washed again.

I thank God for Manna 101. It's the best class anyone could ever take. I can remember my first day in Manna 101. I was scared. It's hard losing all the comforts we are so used to, having to learn how to depend on God and not on ourselves anymore. Like Paul said, we should not have confidence in the flesh. Manna 101 surely makes you understand that there should never be confidence in the flesh.

> ***Romans 7:18 For I know that in me (that is, in my flesh,) dwelleth no good thing: for to will is present with me; but how to perform that which is good I find not.***

I don't know about others, but as for me and my house when I began to eat and live off manna it built my faith. I began to see that I was no longer in Egypt. I knew that I was no longer entangled with the yoke of bondage. When I began to see manna rain down from heaven I asked just like the children of Israel, "What is this?" I can say with all sincerity that the Lord is a keeper. Not only is He a keeper, He is a provider. The Lord provided for me during my manna season. These are the things that my best friend Jackie and I always laugh about how my clothes and shoes never wore out. The Lord sustained everything about me except my perspective on life.

The Lord began to deal with me regarding the pride I had acquired while in Pharaoh's house. The attitude that everything I had was because of me. My grandmother had trusted me with thousands of dollars of credit and like most people I abused the responsibility while in Egypt. I began to go down the wrong path and I began over spending. When the Lord enrolled me in Manna 101 all of that began to change. My grandmother took the credit cards from me and for the first time I was without money or credit. I had to now lean on the everlasting arms and hold onto God's unchanging hand. When I was delivered out of Egypt, the Lord drowned some of my problems in the Red Sea. Some of the friends I could have called on for help was under that same sea. Some of the people I could have called on for help were not to be found.

Why was this? The Lord wanted to show me that I was not in Egypt anymore. In order for me to learn that I was no longer in Egypt all the paths to Egypt had to be cut off. When you think about the children of Israel being delivered from Egypt and how the Egyptians followed them and were drowned in the Red Sea, you can begin to see where the Lord has delivered you from some people and situations. Some of the people you look back at, it was almost impossible to serve the Lord the way you needed to. In Pharaoh's house you weren't able to serve God the way you needed to. You had to listen to the demands and follow the requests of that master. Now you are in the wilderness and you find yourself enrolled in Manna 101.

The difference between us and the children of Israel is that they were all enrolled together. We oftentimes find ourselves in the ship by ourselves. We have found ourselves many times the captain and the crew of the ship of our destiny. Many times we look for someone to board the ship with us. No one is lined up to go on a ship that looks like it's going down. If you could have told the people that the Titanic would sink they wouldn't have boarded that ship. No one is lined up waiting to suffer. A lot of times we want to be delivered from Egypt, but we don't want to endure the wilderness. I have news for you… it's not going to be like that.

> *1 Peter 5:10 But the God of all grace, who hath called us unto his eternal glory by Christ Jesus, after that ye have suffered a while, make you perfect, stablish, strengthen, settle you.*

I love this scripture because it talks about what I believe the Lord was doing in the wilderness with the children of Israel. He was perfecting them through the adversity they were facing and establishing them as a great nation to follow in the footsteps of their father of faith Abraham. I believe He was strengthening them through the Manna and getting ready to settle them in the Promised Land. Hallelujah! Amen to that! I receive that for myself in Jesus name!

This is what the Lord wants to do in your life. He didn't call you into the wilderness to leave you there or call you out of bondage to live a life of fear. After all, you were already a slave to sin, but while you were in your sin you didn't feel like you were suffering. That's why it seems so hard to understand the suffering of your manna season, but Peter helps us out in this area.

> **1 Peter 4:1 Forasmuch then as Christ hath suffered for us in the flesh, arm yourselves likewise with the same mind: for he that hath suffered in the flesh hath ceased from sin;**

Peter tells us to arm ourselves likewise. In other words, get ready to suffer. Jesus suffered for us, what makes us any different? We expect everything to be a cake walk. Some of my greatest trials came after I had received the Lord Jesus into my life. I can also attest that some of my greatest tests came after I began to proclaim the Gospel, but you know what, the devil is a liar and the father of lies. The devil wants us to stop testifying. The devil wants us to remain in the state we were in when we first entered into Manna 101. He wants us to think God is punishing us. The rain falls on the just and the unjust meaning that the weather has changed in your life. You have to reflect on what Paul has said and learn how to be abound and how to be abased. So many of us like to be abounding, but we don't like to be abased.

Suffering to the Christian is like lifting weights and training for a boxer. It is preparing us for the battle.

> *I Corinthians 9:24-27 NLT* ²⁴ *Don't you realize that in a race everyone runs, but only one person gets the prize? So run to win!* ²⁵ *All athletes are disciplined in their training. They do it to win a prize that will fade away, but we do it for an eternal prize.* ²⁶ *So I run with purpose in every step. I am not just shadowboxing.* ²⁷ *I discipline my body like an athlete, training it to do what it should. Otherwise, I fear that after preaching to others I myself might be disqualified.*

What was Paul saying? I'm an athlete in this Christian walk. I prepare myself daily. No doubt in one of his training sessions he encountered Manna 101 preparing him for life. If you listen to God in your manna season He will provide a way out of the wilderness and into the Promised Land according to His will.

> *I Corinthians 10:13 NLT The temptations in your life are no different from what others experience. And God is faithful. He will not allow the temptation to be more that you can stand. When you are tempted, he will show you a way out so that you can endure.*

Paul is saying that when you find yourself in a place where you are tempted to go astray, like in the wilderness, the Lord has made a way for you to endure it. I love this because this means the Lord is always thinking of you and has His eyes on you. Trust me, when you find yourself eating on manna you can rest assured that you are no longer in Egypt because manna is miracle food. Manna is your sure sign that the Lord has delivered you from the Egypt in your life. Rejoice because God has delivered from the yoke of bondage. The Lord has heard your cry and has answered your secret prayer. The Lord is faithful. Keep your trust in Him. Just know God has delivered you out of your present situation and is taking you to the Promised Land. The amount of time you spend in your wilderness is based upon how fast you advance in the class. This is an instructor led, self-paced class, where you determine the end date. Believe it or not it was the children of Israel's fault they remained roaming in the wilderness those 40 years.

How long have you been in your wilderness? What things have you done to make your wilderness experience last longer than it should? Are there areas in your life where you have not allowed God to move on your behalf? Are there areas in your life where you still don't trust God? Do you believe that your manna season has lasted longer than it should have? Look closely at your walk and see if you have learned all the lessons you believe the Lord is trying to show you. Say this prayer:

Dear Lord in the Name of Jesus. I thank you for allowing me to go through the wilderness. I thank you for my manna season. Lord I ask you to search me and if you find anything in me that is hindering my blessing I ask that you take it out of me right now in Jesus Name. I ask you Lord God to shorten my journey through the wilderness by teaching me to depend on you. Lord I will no longer live off your manna but Lord I will begin to live off your word. I will begin to take you at your word. I will begin to trust you with my whole heart. Lord I know that you have destined me for greatness. I know that my promised land is only a few days journey away. I know that you have delivered me from Egypt for purpose. Lord I thank you for preparing me for the School of Life so that I can be an example to others. Lord I thank you that you are going to turn every test of mine in this wilderness into a testimony in Jesus Name and you dear Lord will get the glory. Amen.

The Lord is faithful and will answer the prayers of a sincere heart. You must have faith and know that you are no longer in Egypt. After all you are eating God's Manna!

Chapter Nine

Now I Can Depend On God

"Give us this day our daily bread."
Matthew 6:11

The most important lesson you can possibly learn while in your manna season is to depend on the Lord. It's no coincidence that Jesus would preach and tell us to pray for God to give us our daily bread. What was He talking about? Manna! Manna was the children of Israel's daily bread. When you really think about it, the Lord gave them what they said they were in missing that they had in Egypt: flesh and bread.

> ***Exodus 16:3 And the children of Israel said unto them, Would to God we had died by the hand of the LORD in the land of Egypt, when we sat by the flesh pots, and when we did eat bread to the full; for ye have brought us forth into this wilderness, to kill this whole assembly with hunger.***

The Lord heard their murmurings and cries. Many times we cry out to the Lord from the flesh and when God answers our prayers we say, "What is this?" We pretend like God didn't answer our prayers.

> *Exodus 16:7-8* *⁷ And in the morning, then ye shall see the glory of the LORD; for that he heareth your murmurings against the LORD: and what are we, that ye murmur against us? ⁸ And Moses said, This shall be, when the LORD shall give you in the evening flesh to eat, and in the morning bread to the full; for that the LORD heareth your murmurings which ye murmur against him: and what are we? your murmurings are not against us, but against the LORD.*

It's beautiful that the Lord heard their murmurings and sent them flesh in the evening and bread in the morning. Who but God can send something to you in the wilderness? In the wilderness the only person you can depend on is God. Remember Pharaoh and all your other friends are in Egypt or in the Red Sea. I know when you were in Egypt you had to borrow things from others, but in the wilderness all those things don't matter. Now you have another caretaker. You have another shepherd. You have another taskmaster, but I heard the word say that if you work in His vineyard whatsoever is right He would pay you.

> *Matthew 20:4 And said unto them;*
> *Go ye also into the vineyard, and*
> *whatsoever is right I will give you.*
> *And they went their way*

I just thank the Lord that I have signed up with Jesus. You might say is there is a sign on bonus? Yes there is in:

> *Isaiah 43:25 I, even I, am he that*
> *blotteth out thy transgressions for*
> *mine own sake, and will not*
> *remember thy sins.*

The Lord says when you begin to work for me for my sake I have to clean you up. We all need to be washed. This is what the manna season will do for you if you let it. The Lord is not punishing you. He is teaching you to depend on Him. This is why Jesus said, "Give us this day our daily bread." He was referring to more than bread to eat.

> *John 6:49 Your fathers did eat manna*
> *in the wilderness, and are dead.*

What was Jesus saying? If you simply eat only God's manna and not His word you will be spiritually dead. This might be too deep for some people and I may lose some people, but the truth is that you need more than physical bread. You need the bread of God's word. It was due to unbelief that God had to send down manna to prove Himself to them. He also had to prove the children of Israel to Himself.

The Lord is doing this right now in someone's life. He is preparing you for the battle. He knows in this battle you are going to be shut down from Egypt and that there are going to be times when you can't find help anywhere. He knows that your so-called "friends" are going to let you down and your family isn't going to always be there for you. Lastly, He knows that when you need someone almost no one will be there except for God.

As a boot camp teaches a soldier to survive in all types of battles likewise the Lord trains His people. Our battle cry could come out of…

> *Romans 8:28 And we know that all things work together for good to them that love God, to them who are the called according to his purpose.*

The manna season is one of those things that the Lord is using to work together for our good. I declare that after going through your manna season you will be able to say, "thank you Jesus for taking me through this." I can say earnestly that there is going to be a time when you will look back because I heard someone say, "perspective comes in retrospect", meaning looking back you can see clearer. Why is that? Because you have gone through something! If you haven't been through something how can you tell someone about it? This is why Jesus was so instrumental because as the word says He was tempted in all areas.

> *Hebrews 4:15 For we have not an high priest which cannot be touched with the feeling of our infirmities; but was in all points tempted like as we are, yet without sin.*

Our God isn't like Pharaoh. If He tells you to make brick without stray trust me He's done it too. Jesus walked with us and suffered in the flesh.

> **1 Peter 4:1 Forasmuch then as Christ hath suffered for us in the flesh, arm yourselves likewise with the same mind: for he that hath suffered in the flesh hath ceased from sin; That he no longer should live the rest of his time in the flesh to the lusts of men, but to the will of God.**

It's something about that manna period that gets you out of the flesh and back into the will of God. My wife will tell you I hate to ask for directions, but if I notice that I have gotten lost and that I really can't find my way, I will stop and beg for directions. This is what suffering in the flesh will do. Being whipped in the flesh will make you beg for the will of God in your life. After you get tired of roaming the wilderness you begin to trust in the Lord. When you go through the wilderness and live off manna somehow you begin to know that you can depend on God. Why is this important? It is through your manna season wandering in the wilderness where God justifies you.

> *Romans 8:30 Moreover whom he did predestinate, them he also called: and whom he called, them he also justified: and whom he justified, them he also glorified.*

Isn't that something that He predestined you and then called you? Your manna season is simply preparing you for the battle. In the army they have to train the soldiers on how to find food if they are in a place where there isn't any. They begin to learn how to identify what fruits and grasses to eat. They learn how to survive off of insects. This is what your manna season is doing for you. It is preparing you to go through any type of battle and still depend on God.

When you have this lesson down to a science you have just entered your last semester of Manna 101. When you begin to trust wholeheartedly on God He is preparing your diploma. Once you begin to really depend on God He's closed the grade book and has given you some free time. Things will start to get easier in your life. I heard the word say:

> *Deuteronomy 28:1-2 ¹And it shall come to pass, if thou shalt hearken diligently unto the voice of the LORD thy God, to observe and to do all his commandments which I command thee this day, that the LORD thy God will set thee on high above all nations of the earth: ² And all these blessings shall come on thee, and overtake thee, if thou shalt hearken unto the voice of the LORD thy God.*

God never intended this to be a hard thing. All He wants to do is prove you this day and know if you are going to follow His commandments. He has all the blessings at the start line. He's counting! I can hear Him say, "On your marks, Get Set…" He's waiting for you to trust in Him and begin to walk in His statutes so He can set you High on the earth. Then He's going to tell your blessings to "Go!" Then you will find yourself in the Promised Land, eating the overflow of the Lord. Then your manna season will seem but that 11-day journey it was supposed to be next to the glory that is going to be revealed in that Land!

> **Romans 8:18 For I reckon that the sufferings of this present time are not worthy to be compared with the glory which shall be revealed in us.**

I believe Paul was looking at his manna season and realized that God was going to get some glory out of it. I believe Paul was reading the Father's Holy Will and ran across this revelation in it:

> **Romans 8:17 And if children, then heirs; heirs of God, and joint-heirs with Christ; if so be that we suffer with him, that we may be also glorified together.**

I think someone just got it. We are going to be glorified through our sufferings because we have proven to the world that there is no need to compromise to live a good life. You can walk holy before the Lord and you can live up to His statutes. The Lord has given us too much grace to sit here acting like we can't depend on Him. God gives you the manna daily. Your manna may be your bills being paid by a miraculous source. My manna may be someone bringing food to my house. Whatever it is your prayer should be "give me this day my daily bread." The Lord wants you to get up out the flesh.

> ***Romans 8:8 So then they that are in the flesh cannot please God.***

As long as you were in Egypt your flesh was free to get up and walk. There is something about that wilderness experience that makes your flesh weak, but that manna season will make you depend on God. I believe even an atheist calls on God in their manna season. Thank God for Manna from Heaven.

Now looking at our syllabus we have almost completed all of the requirements. In the next chapter we are going to discuss why even through the wilderness and through the manna season some people still don't make it to the Promised Land and find themselves back in Manna 101.

NOW I CAN DEPEND ON GOD

Chapter Ten

Don't Give Up at the Border of the Promised Land

"And the children of Israel did eat manna forty years, until they came to a land inhabited; they did eat manna, until they came unto the borders of the land of Canaan."
Exodus 16:35

So many people have given up on the promises of God because they were no longer being fed manna. They supposed that God had left them; never realizing that they were on the border of the Promised Land and the need for manna was no more. How can we continue to keep the faith in the midst of all of our adversities and through the wilderness? I propose we must strive for perfection laying aside every weight and the sin that so easily besets us. Don't give up at the border of the Promised Land.

Many people themselves have forfeited the blessing of God because they supposed God had forgotten about them. The truth is they no longer needed the manna. When you are on the border of your Promised Land you have to be careful to know when you are eating God's manna and know when the Promised Land is steps away. We have to keep in mind that Moses never got to see the Promised Land.

All the things God did in the wilderness was for the wilderness period. Things such as:

> *Nehemiah 9:15 And gavest them bread from heaven for their hunger, and broughtest forth water for them out of the rock for their thirst, and promisedst them that they should go in to possess the land which thou hadst sworn to give them.*

The Lord provided for the children of Israel all throughout the wilderness. He gave them bread from heaven and water from a rock. He promised them that they would go and possess the land which He gave to them for an inheritance.

The Lord gave them these provisions because of their complaining.

> *Psalm 105:40 The people asked, and he brought quails, and satisfied them with the bread of heaven.*

As the children of Israel wandered the wilderness they were provided supernaturally, just as we are during our manna season. However, we must always remember that once we are at the border of the Promised Land the manna will cease. The manna will cease because there is no need for manna. God has taken you to the Promised Land.

If you haven't had manna for a while, rejoice, because this means you are very close to your Promised Land. You are about to graduate from Manna 101 and enter into the School of Life.

Chapter Eleven

Graduation from Manna 101

"Moses my servant is dead; now therefore arise, go over this Jordan, thou, and all this people, unto the land which I do give to them, even to the children of Israel."

Joshua 1:2

Now let's pick up from chapter one. We have been in Manna 101 and we have learned the lessons the teacher has laid out for us. We have checked our syllabus and we're almost done.

The teacher begins to tell you that you've done a great job. She tells you that there were times during the class that she didn't know if she was going to be able to pass you. She informs you that she noticed in the beginning you lost faith a few times, but was glad to see that you regained it. She goes on to assure you that you're almost ready to walk into your Promised Land. She recites this scripture:

> ***Joshua 1:6-7** **6** **Be strong and of a good courage: for unto this people shalt thou divide for an inheritance the land, which I sware unto their fathers to give them. **7** Only be thou strong and very courageous, that thou mayest observe to do according to all the law, which Moses my servant commanded thee: turn not from it to the right hand or to the left, that thou mayest prosper withersoever thou goest.*

She reminds you that if you don't do this you may find yourself having to take a refresher course, but don't worry because as long as you have faith in God you will be alright.

What is a refresher course in Manna 101? It means that while you are living your life you might just find yourself back in the classroom again as I did. I should have been the teacher, but I needed to be taught again.

The teacher asks you to stand up. As you stand up, suddenly lights come on all over the building, you glance to the right and to the left and behind you and notice that the entire time you were in a room full of students. Everyone is pleasantly surprised. You were never alone. The teacher laughs and you realize she wasn't as tall as you thought and the class wasn't as hard as you thought it would be.

The teacher says that she would like to congratulate all of you for a job well done. You look around the class and take comfort to know that you weren't there by yourself. After all you see your neighbor who you thought had it so good. You see your Pastor and a bunch of other people you know. You see faces you don't recognize as well. You realize that Manna 101 was truly a Prerequisite to the School of Life. Everyone is laughing and talking and the teacher interrupts. She says, "Now class remember everything you have learned because this was to prepare you for life." You ask her is there a final exam and she tells you that once you had total faith in God you were a graduate.

As you watch her next move, she is writing down names on a large chalkboard. You look at the engravings on the board and it reads…

> *Hebrews 11:1-2 ¹Now faith is the substance of things hoped for, the evidence of things not seen. ² For by it the elders obtained a good report.*

The Hall of Faithers

Excerpts from Hebrews 11

Abel offered unto God a more excellent sacrifice than Cain; Enoch was translated that he should not see death; Noah, being warned of God of things not seen as yet, moved with fear, prepared an ark to the saving of his house; Abraham, when he was called to go out into a place which he should after receive for an inheritance, obeyed; and he went out, not knowing whither he went;

Sara herself received strength to conceive seed, and was delivered of a child when she was past age, because she judged him faithful who had promised. These all died in faith, not having received the promises, but having seen them afar off, and were persuaded of them, and embraced them, and confessed that they were strangers and pilgrims on the earth.

Rahab perished not with them that believed not, when she had received the spies with peace. And what shall I more say? for the time would fail me to tell of Gedeon, and of Barak, and of Samson, and of Jephthae; of David also, and Samuel, and of the prophets: Who through faith subdued kingdoms, wrought righteousness, obtained promises, stopped the mouths of lions. Quenched the violence of fire, escaped the edge of the sword, out of weakness were made strong, waxed valiant in fight, turned to flight the armies of the aliens. Women received their dead raised to life again: and others were tortured, not accepting deliverance; that they might obtain a better resurrection: And others had trial of cruel mockings and scourgings, yea, moreover of bonds and imprisonment: They were stoned, they were sawn asunder, were tempted, were slain with the sword: they wandered about in sheepskins and goatskins; being destitute, afflicted, tormented; (Of whom the world was not worthy:) they wandered in deserts, and in mountains, and in dens and caves of the earth. And these all, having obtained a good report through faith, received not the promise: God having provided some better thing for us, that they without us should not be made perfect.

You realize that this is excerpts from Hebrews 11 and the hall of faithers. Down the list of names and accomplishments you see your name and under your name you see graduate of Manna 101.

Chapter Twelve

Jesus is That Manna

"Then said they unto him Lord, evermore give us this bread."

John 6:34

After all is said and done we have to understand the spiritual implications of manna. Jesus Christ is that manna from heaven. While in the wilderness I keep saying over and over again that the children of Israel ate God's manna but they didn't eat His word.

> *John 6:32-33* [32] *Then Jesus said unto them, Verily, verily, I say unto you, Moses gave you not that bread from heaven; but my Father giveth you the true bread from heaven.* [33] *For the bread of God is he which cometh down from heaven, and giveth life unto the world.*

Even in the wilderness the children of Israel had a chance to experience God's love. Jesus is that true manna. Not being able to get what you want makes you understand that everything you have belongs to the Lord. Jesus is saying that He is the manna that came down from heaven to give life to the world. The Lord is standing there with one position and that is with His arms open wide ready to receive you unto Himself.

> *John 6:37 All that the Father giveth me shall come to me; and him that cometh to me I will in no wise cast out.*

If the Lord has called you out of Egypt it is for a reason. There were some hard taskmasters there. Drugs, sex and sin are hard taskmasters. He has called you out of Egypt for purpose. He has called you into the wilderness to prove you and Himself. He has called you into Manna 101 to show you some new ways of living.

Now if you don't believe me that Jesus is bread for us then I encourage to you search the scriptures.

> *John 6:39-47 ³⁹ Search the scriptures; for in them ye think ye have eternal life: and they are they which testify of me. ⁴⁰ And ye will not come to me, that ye might have life. ⁴¹ I receive not honour from men. ⁴² But I know you, that ye have not the love of God in you. ⁴³ I am come in my Father's name, and ye receive me not: if another shall come in his own name, him ye will receive. ⁴⁴ How can ye believe, which receive honour one of another, and seek not the honour that cometh from God only? ⁴⁵ Do not think that I will accuse you to the Father: there is one that accuseth you, even Moses, in whom ye trust. ⁴⁶ For had ye believed Moses, ye would have believed me; for he wrote of me. ⁴⁷ But if ye believe not his writings, how shall ye believe my words?*

The Lord is knocking right now in the heart of someone.

> *Revelation 3:20 Behold, I stand at the door, and knock: if any man hear my voice, and open the door, I will come in to him, and will sup with him, and he with me.*

God wants to be the lover of your soul and wants to take you out of Egypt. If you look at your map you will find that the wilderness is the shortest way to your Promised Land. You will notice that there isn't anything out there to eat. You had to leave Egypt so fast you really didn't have time to pack for a long journey because you were running for your life! This is what we are doing as Paul said running a race. We are trying to win and by faith we will.

Will you eat only God's manna? Will you continue to let yourself be a third and fourth time repeat of manna 101? You've seen people always in the same situation, stuck for 40 years? You know about the children of Israel. I encourage you to look at your brethren and see what you can correct in your life by observing what was done wrong in theirs'.

John 6:48 I am that bread of life.

Jesus is that bread of life. He is the true manna from heaven. He is the one that God has sent to fill your heart and soul. Don't get stuck like the children of Israel eating only God's Manna!

> *John 6:49 Your fathers did eat manna in the wilderness, and are dead.*

Man cannot live on bread alone and we know this. It's something about soul food that makes you feel good.

> *John 6:50-51 [50] This is the bread which cometh down from heaven, that a man may eat thereof, and not die. [51] I am the living bread which came down from heaven: if any man eat of this bread, he shall live for ever: and the bread that I will give is my flesh, which I will give for the life of the world.*

Jesus is manna. But what was Jesus also?

> *John 1:1 In the beginning was the Word, and the Word was with God, and the Word was God.*

Jesus is the Word. This is why you can't get caught eating only God's manna you have to eat His Word. You have to receive Jesus into your heart.

> *John 6:53 Then Jesus said unto them, Verily, verily, I say unto you, Except ye eat the flesh of the Son of man, and drink his blood, ye have no life in you.*

I ask you today have you partaken of the free meal of salvation? Have you allowed Jesus into your life? Have you allowed the Lord to move you from Egypt into the Promised Land? Are you stuck somewhere in between in a place called the wilderness? Where are you at this level of your walk? Where would you define you walk in the Lord? Have you began to walk with the Lord? Have you been only eating God's Manna?

> *John 6:58 This is that bread which came down from heaven: not as your fathers did eat manna, and are dead: he that eateth of this bread shall live forever.*

Jesus is the bread from heaven. Jesus is that manna we read about. The bible is clear and it tells us what we need to do. Romans 10:9 says *That if thou shalt confess with thy mouth the Lord Jesus, and shalt believe in thine heart that*

God hath raised him from the dead, thou shalt be saved.

So if you aren't saved, say this prayer: Father, in the name of Jesus I pray that you forgive me of my sins. Lord I believe that Jesus is that manna. Lord I believe as the word says that if I eat of His flesh I shall have everlasting life. Lord I believe that the Lord Jesus was crucified for my sins. I believe that He died and with His death my sins were buried with Him. Lord I believe in my heart that you rose Him again from the dead and that when He rose I rose again too. Lord I thank you in Jesus name for accepting me into your fold. Lord I know that Jesus is the Good Shepherd and Lord I pray that I only hear your voice in Jesus Name. Amen.

If you said that prayer and meant it in your heart, I want to be the first to welcome you into the Kingdom of God. I'll see you in Heaven! Your next step is to find you a good bible teaching church, where the word of God is being taught so that you can grow in the Lord.

EPILOGUE

DON'T GIVE UP ON GOD'S PROMISE

Many of us have given up on the promises of God because of unbelief. We get into a place where we begin to think that God is not going to be able to accomplish this task. Sometimes we think that God has forgotten about the promise that He has made us. I have to remind you that all the promises of God are yea and amen! You don't have to wonder if it's going to come to pass. You can just wait for the manifestation of His glory to be revealed in you. One thing I've learn is God is faithful. He will stick closer than any brother. He's there when you need Him. He's more reliable than your mother or father. No matter what you think, God loves you, you and especially YOU!

This chapter is unnumbered because one thing I have learned about Manna 101 is that you make it as long or as short as you want it to be! When I wrote this book I printed it out and placed it in an envelope and for over 6 years it remained in that envelope. Many of you reading this book have done exactly that with your gifts and talents. You have allowed so much time to pass and you have allowed those things to remain sealed up somewhere. I am believing that you will learn that your manna season is only a season and seasons change! Don't get discouraged because God is with you! Don't allow anything to stop your faith.

Since this book was written I've been licensed in ministry, ordained and founded a church and God has proven Himself faithful. I chose not to rewrite the book because I wanted the book to capture the spirit of that season in my life. I almost didn't want to share my experience in the wilderness but I realized that it's vital to our growth as

Christians to know that others are in the wilderness with us. I let a few people who were close to me read it and they encouraged me that I had to release this book. Even when I would tell people the ideas behind the book they would tell me to release it! It is my prayer that God has truly touched you through the words of this book. It is my fervent hope that you will receive the promise. I'm praying that just as I did you learn the power of your manna season and embrace Manna 101: The Prerequisite to the School of Life!

I pray your strength in the Lord, even so, come Lord Jesus. Amen.

Apostle Dontez Williams

www.ingramcontent.com/pod-product-compliance
Lightning Source LLC
LaVergne TN
LVHW052255070426
835507LV00035B/2910